SHARK SEARCH

In Search of
Tiger Sharks

Shaye Reynolds

PowerKiDS
press

New York

Published in 2016 by The Rosen Publishing Group, Inc.
29 East 21st Street, New York, NY 10010

First Edition

Editor: Caitie McAneney
Book Design: Mickey Harmon

Photo Credits: Cover, p. 1 (iron bars) Wayne Lynch/All Canada Photos/Getty Images; cover, pp. 1, 3, 4, 6, 8, 10, 12, 14, 16, 18, 20–24 (background) Ase/Shutterstock.com; cover (tiger shark), p. 7 (inset) Luiz Felipe V. Puntel/Shutterstock.com; pp. 5, 7 (main), 9 (main), 11, 20 Matt9122/Shutterstock.com; p. 9 (inset) Jim Abernethy/National Geographic/Getty Images; p. 13 Image Source/Getty Images; pp. 15, 22 Greg Amptman/Shutterstock.com; p. 17 © Andre Seale / Alamy Stock Photo; p. 19 (beach) tratong/Shutterstock.com; p. 19 (sign) mingis/Shutterstock.com; p. 19 (sign post) Alesandro14/Shutterstock.com; p. 19 (inset) Jim Agronick/Shutterstock.com.

Library of Congress Cataloging-in-Publication Data

Reynolds, Shaye, author.
 In search of tiger sharks / Shaye Reynolds.
    pages cm. — (Shark search)
 Includes index.
 ISBN 978-1-5081-4347-5 (pbk.)
 ISBN 978-1-5081-4348-2 (6 pack)
 ISBN 978-1-5081-4349-9 (library binding)
 1. Tiger shark—Juvenile literature. 2. Tiger shark—Behavior—Juvenile literature. [1. Sharks.] I. Title.
 QL638.95.C3R49 2016
 597.3'4—dc23
                              2015027134

Manufactured in the United States of America

CPSIA Compliance Information: Batch #BW16PK: For Further Information contact Rosen Publishing, New York, New York at 1-800-237-9932

Contents

Swimming with the Tiger Shark............ 4

Identifying a Tiger Shark................ 6

Helpful Body Parts...................... 8

Amazing Senses........................ 10

Scary Scavengers.......................12

Roaming the Coasts....................14

Tiger Shark Pups...................... 16

Shark Attack! 18

Sharks in Danger...................... 20

Respect for the Tiger Shark 22

Glossary 23

Index................................. 24

Websites.............................. 24

Swimming with the Tiger Shark

The tiger shark is known by many names. Many call it the sea tiger, while others call it the leopard shark, spotted shark, and even man-eater. It earned the first three names for the striped and spotted pattern on young tiger sharks. It earned the name "man-eater" for its bloody attacks on people.

If you're swimming in waters known for tiger sharks, be on the lookout. Read on to learn more about tiger sharks!

Tiger sharks are **scavengers** and will eat nearly anything they can find. Luckily, people aren't the number one item on a tiger shark's menu.

Identifying a Tiger Shark

How can you **identify** a tiger shark? They're easily set apart from other sharks. That's because most sharks have pointed **snouts**. Instead, tiger sharks have a snout that's squared in front. They usually grow to around 14 feet (4.3 meters) long, but some are even bigger.

Young tiger sharks are easy to identify. That's because they have dark stripes and spots on their back. The stripes fade as the shark gets older. Adult tiger sharks are gray or dark blue on top and white or cream colored on their underside.

If you see a big shark in the water, look at its skin. Its coloring may help you identify what kind of shark it is.

young tiger shark's stripes

Helpful Body Parts

Tiger sharks are well **adapted** to their ocean **habitat**. They have fins to help them swim. There are two pectoral fins where arms would be. They have two fins on top called dorsal fins. Tiger sharks also have two fins on their underside and one on their tail called the caudal fin.

Tiger sharks have large, sharp teeth with jagged edges like a knife. The tip of each tooth is bent backward, which helps them hold on to their **prey**. They also have a set of very powerful jaws.

A tiger shark's sharp teeth and strong jaws allow it to eat shelled animals, such as clams. They can even crack the huge shells of sea turtles!

dorsal fins

caudal fin

anal fin

pelvic fin

pectoral fins

Amazing Senses

Sharks have been around for millions of years. In that time, they've **developed** supersenses to help them survive and hunt. Tiger sharks have eyes that can see well even in dim conditions, such as deep and **murky** water. They have a great sense of smell, which helps them locate prey.

Tiger sharks can also sense electrical fields to help them find prey. They have a strong sense of the movement around them. These sharks are built for the hunt!

A tiger shark's supersenses make it a great scavenger.

11

Scary Scavengers

Tiger sharks are **aggressive** hunters who will eat nearly anything. Unlike many other sharks, they don't care what something tastes like. They'll go after large sea **mammals**, such as seals and dolphins. They'll also hunt sea snakes, squids, and stingrays. Fish, other sharks, and even birds are on this shark's menu.

Tiger sharks also eat trash. Scientists and fishermen have found many objects in the stomachs of dead tiger sharks, such as cans, bottles, and even tires.

Another nickname for the tiger shark is "wastebasket of the sea." That's because it'll eat anything it finds—even trash!

13

Roaming the Coasts

The bad news for swimmers is that tiger sharks live in coastal waters around the world. These waters are full of prey for sharks to hunt. Tiger sharks are even found in harbors and river **estuaries**. Central Pacific islands are also home to a large population of tiger sharks.

Tiger sharks prefer tropical waters, which are warm. They **migrate** to cooler waters in the summer and return to tropical waters in the winter.

Tiger sharks like to live in murky waters. They can use their supersenses to find prey and sneak up on it.

tiger shark range

Tiger Shark Pups

Tiger sharks give birth to many babies at once. Their babies are called pups. Unlike most fish and other sharks, tiger sharks don't lay eggs. Instead, they give birth to live babies. Mother sharks hold their growing pups inside of them for 14 to 16 months. In that time, the pups might eat each other and unused eggs inside their mother's body. They're hunters from the start!

A mother tiger shark will give birth to between 10 and 80 pups. That's a lot of sharks!

Tiger shark pups are around 1 foot (0.3 m) long when they're born. They have dark stripes and spots on their skin.

Shark Attack!

Many people have heard about the great white shark, which is known to attack swimmers and surfers. While the great white is the number one man-eater, the tiger shark is a close second.

While great whites may take a bite, they often let go. They don't like the taste of people and would rather eat seals or sea lions. Tiger sharks will eat anything, though—even people. They're less likely to let go, which makes them deadly.

Hawaiian spear fisherman Braxton Roca was attacked by a tiger shark on September 20, 2015. The shark bit his leg and wouldn't let go! It finally let go after Roca punched the shark's snout.

great white shark

SHARK
SIGHTED
TODAY

ENTER WATER
AT OWN
RISK

Sharks in Danger

Tiger sharks are an important part of their **ecosystem** because they eat many animals and keep their populations from becoming too large. These hunters are in danger, though. While they might hurt humans occasionally, humans are a much greater risk to them.

People like to fish for tiger sharks as a sport. They also hunt tiger sharks for their skin and fins. Some catch tiger sharks for their liver, which is full of vitamin A, to use in vitamins. Tiger sharks are considered "near threatened," which means their populations may be at risk of dropping soon.

Shark Bites!

 The biggest tiger sharks can weigh more than 2,000 pounds (907 kg).

 Tiger sharks may live up to 50 years in the wild.

 Tiger sharks hunt alone and at night.

 Tiger sharks swim slowly to keep prey from noticing them.

 There have only been 111 confirmed cases of tiger sharks attacking people for no reason since 1580.

Respect for the Tiger Shark

Because of overfishing, tiger sharks are in trouble. Why would we try to save a man-eating shark? These supersharks have a bad **reputation**, but there are only a few attacks each year. Most tiger sharks stick to eating ocean creatures.

Tiger sharks are amazing animals that have been roaming Earth's oceans for millions of years. They have supersenses and bodies built for the hunt. It's important to respect this shark and hope you never cross paths.

Glossary

adapt: Change to fit new conditions.

aggressive: Showing a readiness to attack.

develop: To grow and change over time.

ecosystem: All the living things in an area.

estuary: An area where the ocean's tide meets a river.

habitat: The natural home for plants, animals, and other living things.

identify: To tell what something is.

mammal: A warm-blooded animal that has a backbone and hair, breathes air, and feeds milk to its young.

migrate: To move from one area to another for feeding or having babies.

murky: Very dark or foggy.

prey: An animal hunted by other animals for food.

reputation: The views that are held about something or someone.

scavenger: An animal that eats what it can find, including waste and dead animals.

snout: An animal's nose and mouth.

Index

B
babies, 16

C
caudal fin, 8, 9
coastal waters, 14
colors, 6

D
dorsal fins, 8, 9

E
ecosystem, 20
eggs, 16

F
fins, 8, 9, 20

H
habitat, 8

J
jaws, 8

M
menu, 4, 12

N
names, 4

O
overfishing, 22

P
pectoral fins, 8, 9
people, 4, 18,
     20, 21
prey, 8, 10, 14, 21
pups, 16

S
scavengers, 4, 10
snout, 6
stripes and spots,
     6, 16
supersenses, 10,
     14, 22

T
teeth, 8, 9
trash, 12
tropical waters, 14

W
wastebasket of the
     sea, 12

Websites

Due to the changing nature of Internet links, PowerKids Press has developed an online list of websites related to the subject of this book. This site is updated regularly. Please use this link to access the list: www.powerkidslinks.com/search/tiger